DIY JEWELRY

LEARN THE BASICS

Making your own jewelry is amazingly easy! Beginning on page 4, you'll find the quick and fun basics on determining necklace lengths, choosing beads, and exploring findings (jewelry hardware) and tools. After that, eight techniques are introduced with skill-building projects to let you practice what you've just learned! You'll breeze through stringing beads, making pendants, using chain, and so much more! This exciting hobby has never been simpler or more rewarding!

LEISURE ARTS, INC.
Maumelle, Arkansas

CONTENTS

JEWELRY MAKING BASICS

Welcome to the wonderful world of jewelry making! You'll love wearing and sharing jewelry that you've created. This leaflet will teach you all the basics.

First, you'll learn about a wide array of bead types. Then, you'll explore the findings—from chain to leather and bead caps to jump rings—that complement the beads. Next up are the tools, those gadgets that bring everything together into a necklace, bracelet, or earrings.

The exciting jewelry projects begin on page 14. Each design builds on the skills & techniques learned in a previous one, but none are difficult, so you can pick any project to start.

Sizing It Up

This table and drawing show various necklace lengths and about where they fall on the body. The lengths are commonly used in the jewelry world, but feel free to adjust your necklaces to suit you and your fashion sense.

Common Jewelry Lengths

Bracelet	6" to 8"
Choker	14" to 16"
Princess	17" to 19"
Matinee	20" to 24"
Opera	28" to 34"
Rope	40" to 45"
Lariat	Over 45"

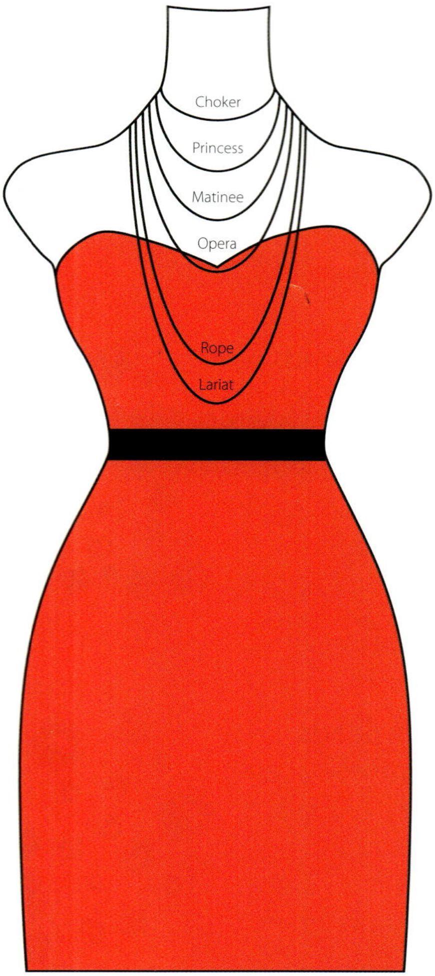

CHOOSING BEADS

Beads come in all sizes, shapes, colors, finishes, and materials.

Ceramic and stone beads come in several shapes and may be glazed or similarly textured.

Glass beads come in all sizes, shapes, and colors. Some have a shiny, polished, or iridescent finish, while others may have a matte finish.

Crystal beads have multiple machine-cut facets that capture and reflect light with lots of sparkle. They come in dozens of colors, sizes, and shapes.

Metal beads, including spacers and spacer beads, can be made of base metal (which is nonprecious) or plated metals.

Faux pearls have a synthetic coating over a crystal, glass, or plastic base. They are very uniform in size, shape, and color.

Plastic or acrylic beads are lightweight and can give a more whimsical look to your jewelry. Some metal-look beads are plastic; others may be highly polished to look like glass.

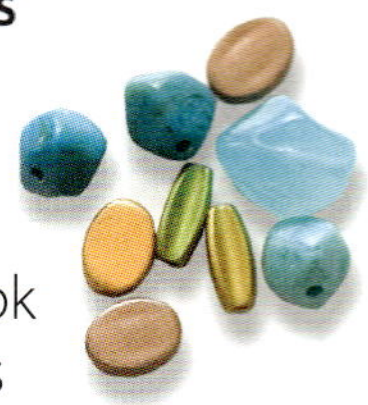

Shell beads have a lustrous finish. They can be uniform in size, shape, and color or be more varied and organic. They can even be actual whole shells!

Seed beads are usually the smallest beads and are available in different sizes, shapes, and colors. This category includes small round beads, small tube beads, bugle beads, and the larger e-beads.

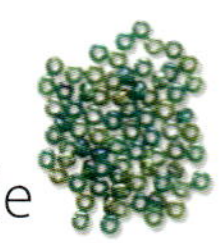

Wood beads give your jewelry a natural, organic look. They are available in many sizes, shapes, and finishes.

CHOOSING FINDINGS

Findings are the components used to assemble jewelry.

Beading thread is strong and has very little stretch. This soft thread easily passes through a beading needle's eye, knots well, and will create a soft, flowing jewelry piece.

Chains come in a variety of sizes, styles, colors, and finishes.

Leather and suede cords come in a variety of sizes and colors and are used for a more casual look.

Nylon-coated beading wire is made up of multiple strands of metal that are twisted together and coated with nylon; the more strands, the stronger and more flexible the wire. It is available in various diameters and strengths.

Stretch cord is great for bracelets and is more durable than thin elastic. A drop of jeweler's glue on the knot will keep the bracelet secure.

Cord is available in many colors and may be cotton, linen, or jute.

Bead caps add texture and sparkle when placed next to beads.

Clasps of all sizes, shapes, and styles are available. Lobster clasps are shaped like a lobster's claw and have a spring-action closure. A toggle clasp is secured by sliding the bar through the loop. There are also spring-ring clasps, hook and eye clasps, box clasps, and magnetic clasps.

Cones are findings that hide the ends of multi-strand jewelry pieces.

Cord ends fit over the ends of ribbon, leather, and cord. They may be crimped and/or glued in place.

Crimp beads or tubes are small metal beads that are flattened over jewelry wire to finish the ends or hold elements in place. The beads are rounded and the tubes are cylinder-shaped. Both come in many sizes and finishes.

Just about any earring style can be made with the wide variety of **ear wires** available–large kidney, fishhook, hoop, pinch bail, etc.

Head pins and eye pins are very similar and are used in similar situations when making jewelry. A head pin is a straight wire with a head of some sort; many are flat, but there are several decorative styles as well. An eye pin is also a straight wire, but it has a loop at one end. This loop may be opened and closed with chain-nose pliers, just like a jump ring.

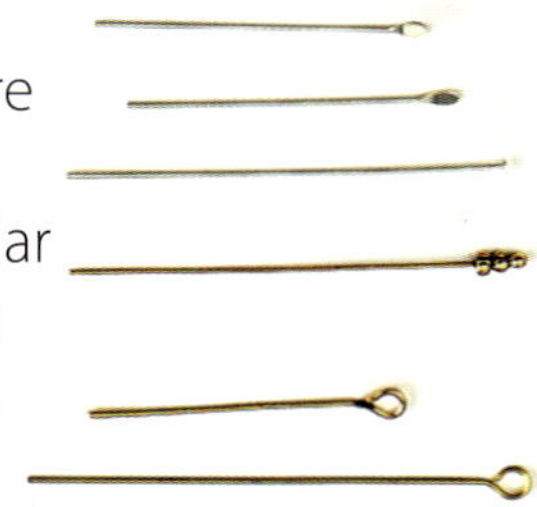

Jump rings are metal rounds or ovals that are used to attach jewelry components to each other. The rings are opened and closed with chain-nose pliers.

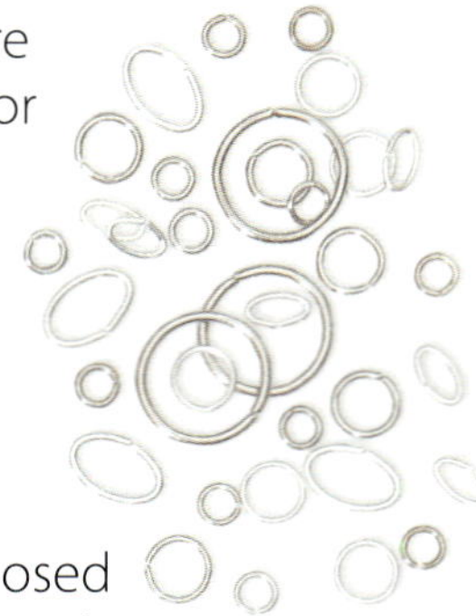

Spacer bars keep beaded strands separate on bracelets and necklaces. Some are very decorative and become a design element, while others are more discreet in their appearance.

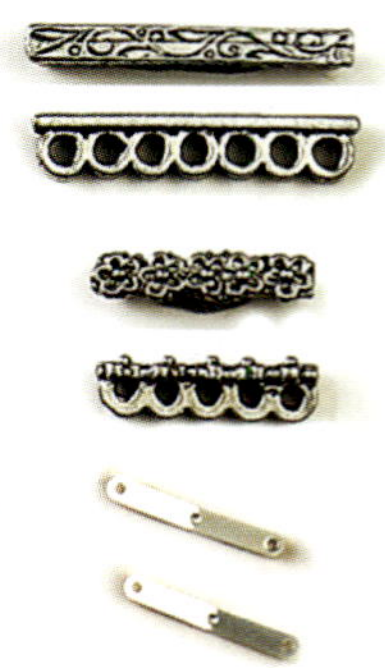

TOOLS & HOW TO USE THEM

The two most common types of **beading needles** are the flexible wire needle and the rigid metal needle. The eye of the flexible wire needle collapses on itself, making it easier to go through small-hole beads.

Bead mats are made of foam-like material and keep the beads from rolling all over the work surface.

Bead boards are very handy. Not only can you see your necklace or bracelet in its final arrangement, the board also has measurements so that you no longer have to guess how many beads you'll need for a specific length.

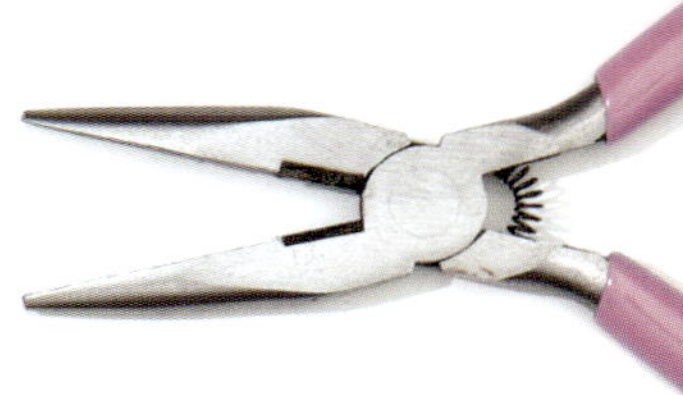

Chain-nose pliers have rounded, tapered jaws and a flat interior surface that will not mar wire or metal findings. These pliers are used for opening and closing jump rings and bending wire. They may also be called needle-nose pliers. You'll need 2 pair to open jump rings and loops on head pins and eye pins.

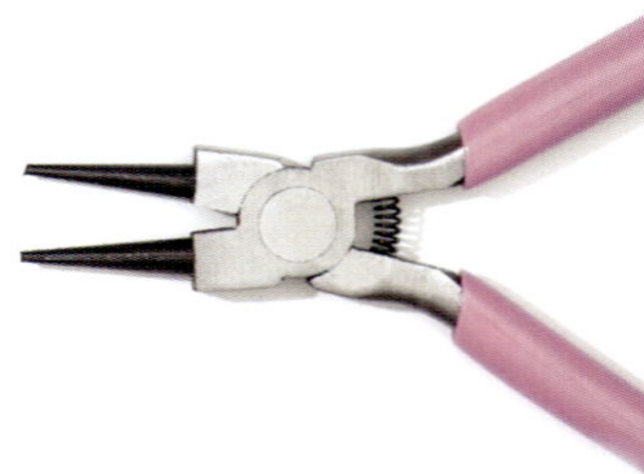

Round-nose pliers have round jaws that are useful for making loops and bending wire smoothly.

Wire cutters are used to cut beading wire, head pins, eye pins, and other soft metals.

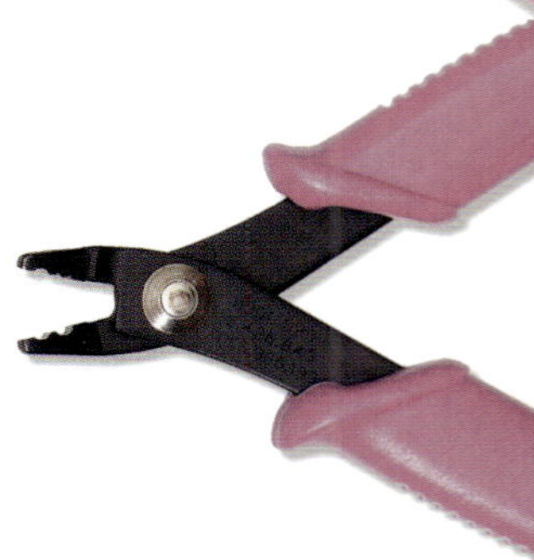

A **crimp tool** (also known as crimping pliers) flattens and shapes the crimp bead or crimp tube.

Spring bead stops keep beads from sliding off when threading beads on beading wire. Just squeeze the ends and slip the wire between the spring coils.

STRINGING BEADS

Stringing beads on a length of stretch cord is the simplest way to make a piece of jewelry. When making these bracelets, you'll learn how to use a bead stop, how to thread beads on stretch cord, and how to secure the bracelet with a surgeon's knot.

STRETCHY BRACELETS

For each bracelet, you'll need:

- assorted medium and small beads (about 33-60)
- a larger, contrasting color bead to act as a bead stop
- stretch cord
- jeweler's glue
- flexible wire beading needle (optional)

You'll also need:

- ribbon

Read Jewelry Making Basics, pages 4-13, before making your bracelets.

To make each bracelet:

1. Cut a 12" length of cord. String the bead stop on one end of the cord; loop the cord around and through the bead stop to hold it in place ***(Fig. 1)***. String the beads for the bracelet on the stretch cord, using a beading needle if desired.

Fig. 1

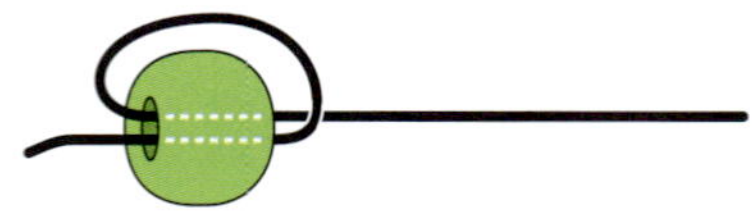

2. Check the bracelet size by carefully wrapping it around your wrist, adding or removing beads until the bracelet fits the way you like. Loosen the cord and carefully remove the bead stop. Tie the cord with a surgeon's knot ***(Fig. 2)*** and apply a drop of glue to the knot. Once dry, trim the cord ends.

Fig. 2

3. Repeat Steps 1 and 2 to make 5 bracelets. Cut a 16" ribbon length. Tie the bracelets together with a ribbon bow.

TWISTY BRACELET

You'll need:

- assorted small crystal and green beads (we used about 537 beads)
- beading thread
- beading needle
- jeweler's glue
- ribbon

Read Jewelry Making Basics, pages 4-13, before making your bracelet.

To make the bracelet:

1. Cut three 31" lengths of beading thread.
2. With a bead stop at one end ***(Fig. 1)***, string beads on each thread length until the beaded section is 18½". Remove the bead stop. Tie each thread with a surgeon's knot ***(Fig. 2)*** and apply a drop of glue to the knot. Once dry, trim the thread ends.

Fig. 1

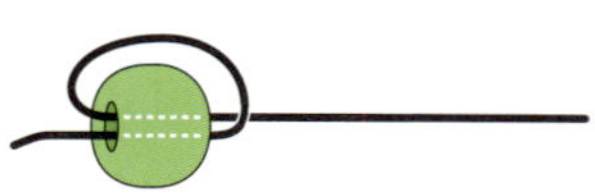

Fig. 2

3. Loop the strands over one finger on each hand. Holding one hand stationary, twist the strands. Thread the ribbon through the loops where your fingers are and tie a bow, making the bracelet.

USING JUMP RINGS

Jump rings are some of the most important findings used when making jewelry. These metal rounds or ovals come in several sizes and metal finishes. They are easily opened and closed with chain-nose pliers, allowing you to add a clasp, charms, pendants, or any other hanging embellishment to your project.

CHARMING BRACELETS

For each bracelet, you'll need:

- assorted medium and small pink, faux pearl, and crystal beads (we used 30-40)
- a larger, contrasting color bead to act as a bead stop
- stretch cord
- jeweler's glue
- flexible wire beading needle (optional)

You'll also need:

- ribbon

For the charm bracelet, you'll also need:

- assorted silver charms (we used 6)
- silver jump rings
- chain-nose pliers (2 pair)

Read Jewelry Making Basics, pages 4-13, before making your bracelets.

To make each bracelet:

1. String the bead stop on one end of a 12" length of cord; loop the cord around and through the bead stop ***(Fig. 1)***. String the beads on the cord, using a beading needle if desired.

Fig. 1

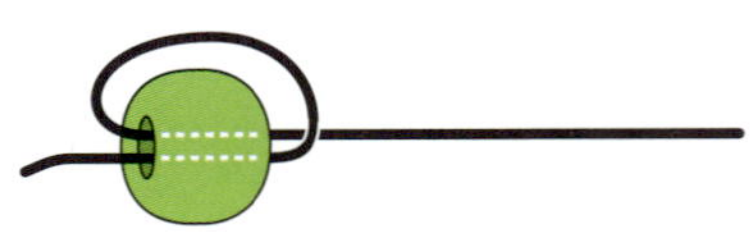

Continued on page 20.

HONG KONG
MOSCOW
LONDON

CHARMING BRACELETS continued

2. Check the size by carefully wrapping it around your wrist, adding or removing beads until the bracelet is the right length. Loosen the cord and remove the bead stop. Tie the cord with a surgeon's knot ***(Fig. 2)*** and apply a drop of glue to the knot. Once dry, trim the cord ends.

Fig. 2

3. To add charms to the bracelet, pick up a jump ring with one pair of the chain-nose pliers. With the second pair of chain-nose pliers, gently hold the other side of the ring. Open the ring by pulling one pair of pliers toward you while pushing the other away ***(Fig. 3)***. Slide the charm on the open ring.

Fig. 3

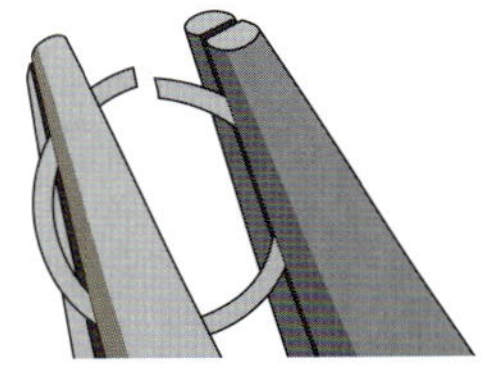

4. While the ring is still open, slip the jump ring on the bracelet cord.
5. Close the jump ring by pushing and pulling the pliers in the opposite direction, bringing the ring ends back together. Add as many charms to your bracelet as you'd like.
6. Tie the bracelets together with a ribbon bow.

CROSS NECKLACE

Approx. length: 22", excluding pendant

You'll need:

- copper cross pendant
- black chain
- black toggle clasp
- 3 black jump rings
- chain-nose pliers (2 pair) and wire cutters

Read Jewelry Making Basics, pages 4-13, before making your necklace.

To make the necklace:

1. Cut a 22" length of chain.
2. Use jump rings ***(Fig. 3, page 20)*** to attach the clasp to the chain ends.
3. Use a jump ring to attach the pendant to the chain.

USING CRIMP BEADS

Crimp beads are small metal beads that are pressed and flattened with a crimp tool, finishing the wire end or holding beads in place. Learning how to use crimp beads also allows you to attach wire to jump rings, clasps, and other objects.

ILLUSION BRACELET

You'll need:

- medium crystal beads (we used 8 green and 8 blue)
- medium silver/rhinestone beads (we used 3)
- small silver textured beads (we used 24)
- small shiny silver beads (we used 4)
- silver seed beads (we used 12)
- silver nylon-coated beading wire
- silver jump rings
- silver toggle clasp
- silver crimp beads and crimp tool
- chain-nose pliers (2 pair) and wire cutters

Read Jewelry Making Basics, pages 4-13, before making your bracelet.

For this bracelet, you'll need to decide the bracelet length ahead of time, taking into account the length of the clasp. Do not add bead groups past this determined length.

Continued on page 24.

ILLUSION BRACELET continued

To make the bracelet:

1. Slide a 20" wire length through a jump ring; center the jump ring on the wire and fold the wire in half. Thread a crimp bead over both wire ends, positioning it near the jump ring. Place the crimp bead on the inner groove of the crimp tool and squeeze ***(Fig. 1)***. Release the tool, turn the crimp bead a quarter turn, and place it in the outer groove ***(Fig. 2)***. Squeeze the tool to round out the crimp bead ***(Fig. 3)***.

Fig. 1

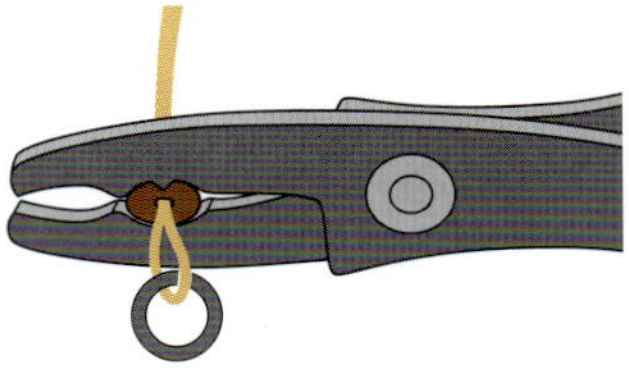

Fig. 2

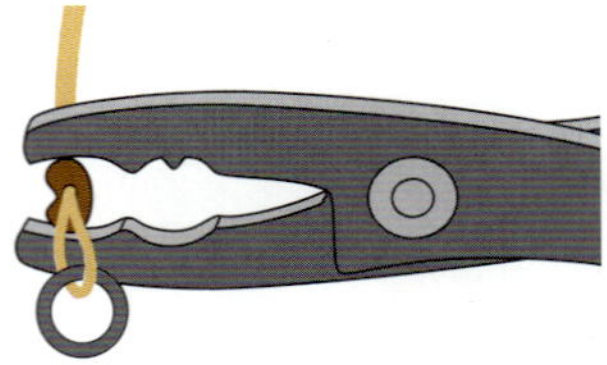

Fig. 3

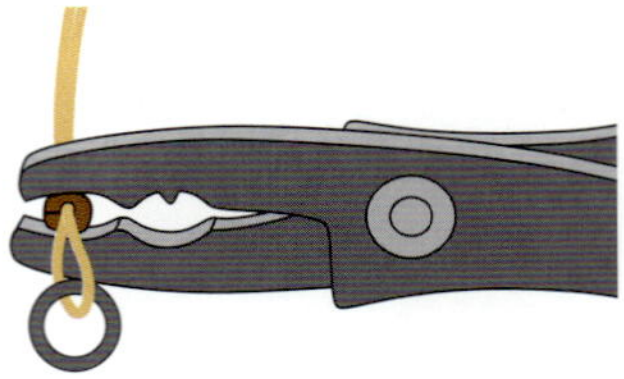

2. Add a second wire length to the jump ring ***(Photo 1)***.

Photo 1

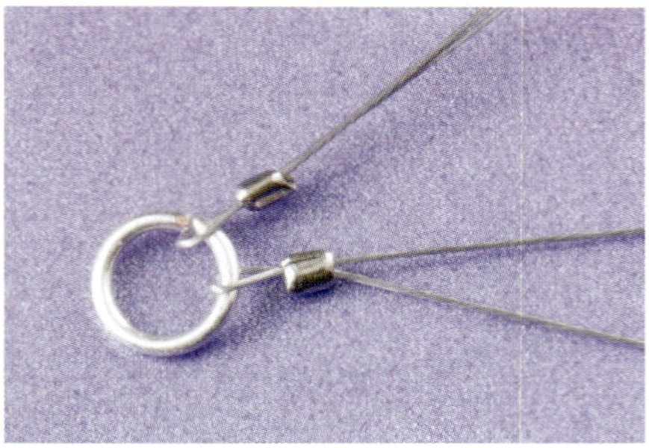

3. For each bead group, thread a crimp bead on a wire and secure. Then thread the beads (3-5) and another crimp bead on the wire. Secure the crimp bead; this will hold the bead group in place. Continue adding bead groups, spacing them along the wires as desired ***(Photo 2)***. Remember not to add bead groups past the determined bracelet length. Add bead groups to all 4 wires.

Photo 2

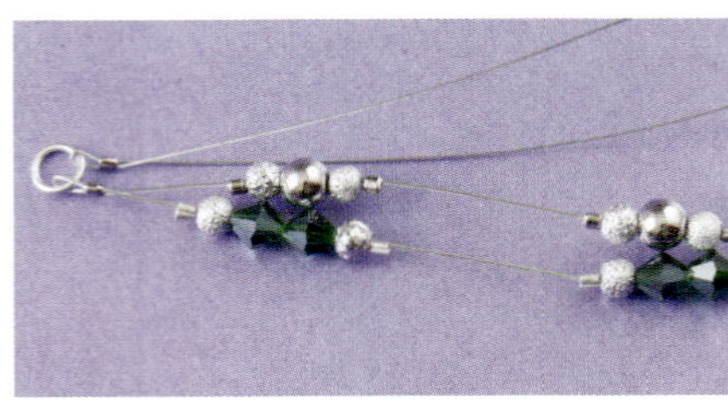

Continued on page 26.

ILLUSION BRACELET continued

4. After all the bead groups are secure, use crimp beads to attach the wire ends to a jump ring ***(Fig. 4)***. Trim the shorter wire ends close to the crimp beads. Attach the clasp to the jump rings ***(Fig. 3, page 20)***.

Fig. 4

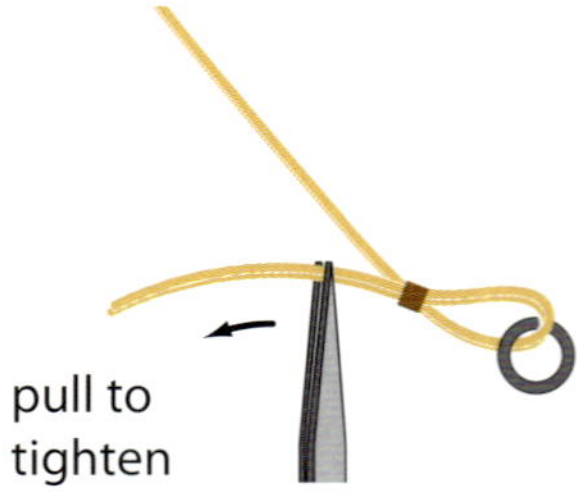

More Info About Crimp Beads

If you are making a beaded bracelet or necklace that has beads all the way to the wire end, you can hide the wire end in the beads. To finish the wire end, thread a crimp bead and the clasp or jump ring on the wire. Run the wire back through the crimp bead and then through several beads ***(Fig. 5)****. Secure the crimp bead and trim the wire end.*

Fig. 5

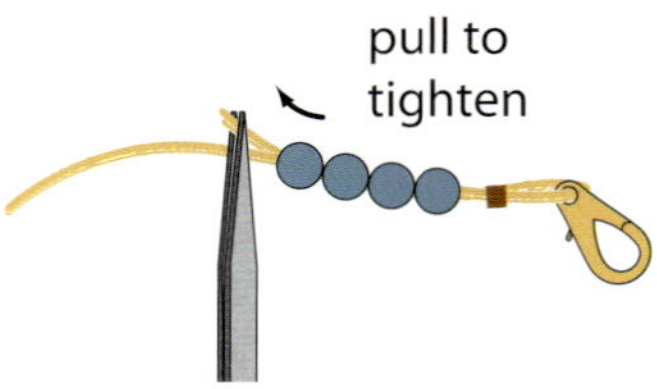

MAKING BEAD DANGLES

A bead dangle consists of a bead (or beads) threaded on a head pin. The head pin is then trimmed and bent to create a loop at the top. This loop can be opened and closed to attach the bead dangle to other components.

CHANDELIER EARRINGS

You'll need:

- 2 gold filigree teardrop shapes
- 2 medium brown beads
- 6 assorted charms (in pairs)
- 2 gold ear wires with attached pinch bails
- 2 gold head pins
- 8 silver jump rings
- chain-nose pliers (2 pair), round-nose pliers, and wire cutters

Read Jewelry Making Basics, pages 4-13, before making your earrings.

For each earring:

1. To make the bead dangle, slide a bead on a head pin. Leaving about 1/2" of wire at the end, cut off the excess wire. Using the chain-nose pliers, bend the wire at a 90° angle ***(Fig. 1)***.

Fig. 1

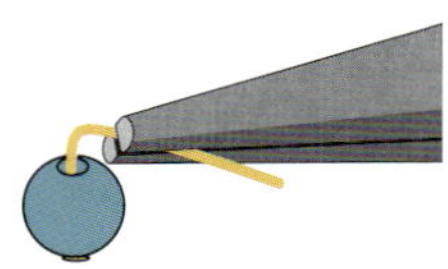

Continued on page 28.

CHANDELIER EARRINGS continued

2. Grasp the wire end with the round-nose pliers. Turn the pliers and bend the wire into a loop ***(Figs. 2-3)***. Release the pliers. Straighten or twist the loop further if necessary.

Fig. 2

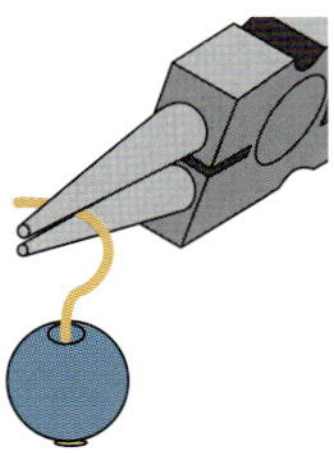

Fig. 3

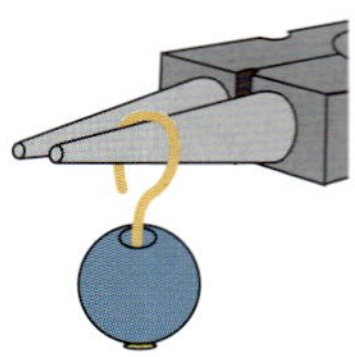

3. Use jump rings ***(Fig. 3, page 20)*** to attach the bead dangle and the charms to the teardrop.
4. Attach the teardrop to the ear wire pinch bail by squeezing the bail closed over the teardrop ***(Fig. 4)***.

Fig. 4

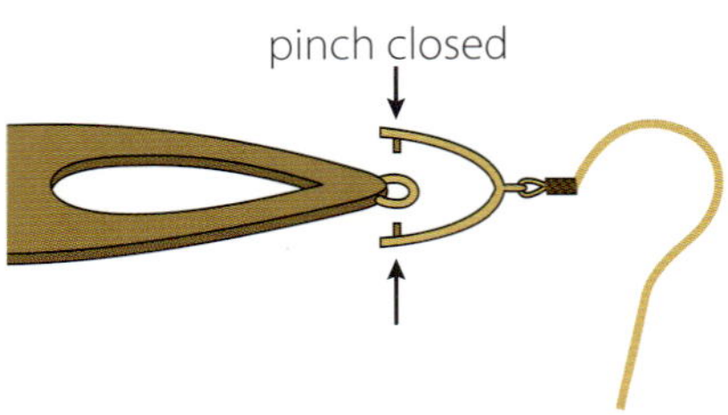

HOOP EARRINGS

You'll need:

- 10 assorted large, medium, and small beads (in pairs)
- 4 silver bead caps
- 2 silver hoop earrings
- 2 silver head pins
- 2 silver jump rings
- chain-nose pliers (2 pair), round-nose pliers, and wire cutters

Read Jewelry Making Basics, pages 4-13, before making your earrings.

For each earring:

1. Make a bead dangle ***(Figs. 1-3, pages 27-28)*** with the beads, bead caps, and a head pin. Attach a jump ring ***(Fig. 3, page 20)*** to the dangle.
2. Slide the dangle on the hoop earring.

MAKING BEADED CONNECTORS

By threading beads on an eye pin and making a loop at the top, you create a beaded connector. These connectors can add length to dangles, join metal links, and can even be joined to each other to make long beaded segments.

PEACE SIGN BRACELET

You'll need:

- medium glass beads (we used 5)
- silver peace sign links (we used 5)
- silver toggle clasp
- silver eye pins
- small and medium silver jump rings
- chain-nose pliers (2 pair), round-nose pliers, and wire cutters

Read Jewelry Making Basics, pages 4-13, before making your bracelet.

To make the bracelet:

1. To make a beaded connector, slide a bead on an eye pin. Leaving about 1/2" of wire at the end, cut off the excess wire. Using the chain-nose pliers, bend the wire at a 90° angle ***(Fig. 1)***.

Fig. 1

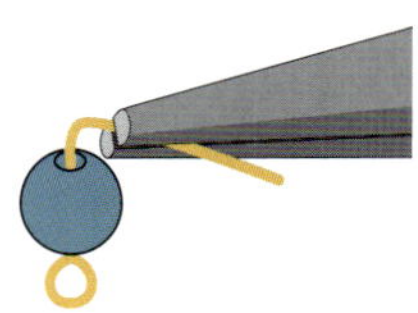

Continued on page 32.

PEACE SIGN BRACELET continued

2. Grasp the wire end with the round-nose pliers. Turn the pliers and bend the wire into a loop ***(Figs. 2-3)***. Release the pliers. Straighten or twist the loop further if necessary. Make 5 beaded connectors. ***(Photo 1)***

Fig. 2

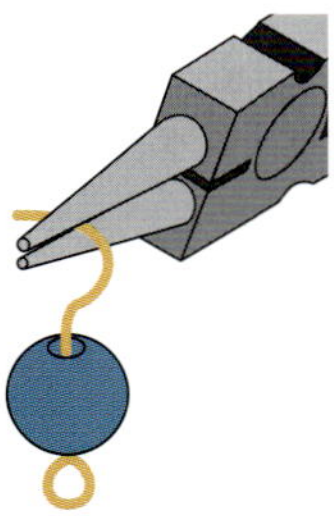

Fig. 3

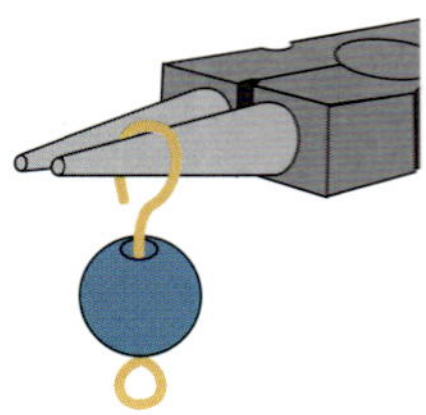

Photo 1

3. Use the small jump rings ***(Fig. 3, page 20)*** to join the beaded connectors and silver peace sign links. Check the bracelet length, adding or removing connectors and/or links until the bracelet is the right length.
4. Attach the clasp to the bracelet with the medium jump rings.

RECTANGLES NECKLACE

Approx. length: 28"

You'll need:

- ◆ large brown plastic open-rectangle beads (we used 11)
- ◆ medium flat round stone beads (we used 10)
- ◆ antique copper large oval jump rings
- ◆ antique copper eye pins
- ◆ antique copper lobster clasp
- ◆ chain-nose pliers (2 pair), round-nose pliers, and wire cutters

Read Jewelry Making Basics, pages 4-13, before making your necklace.

To make the necklace:

1. To make the beaded connector, thread a bead on an eye pin. Make a loop ***(Figs. 1-3, pages 31-32)*** at the wire end ***(Photo 1)***. Make 10 connectors.

Photo 1

2. Beginning and ending with the open-rectangle beads, use jump rings ***(Fig. 3, page 20)*** to join the beads and connectors.
3. Attach jump rings to the end beads. Attach the clasp to one jump ring.

USING CHAIN

Chain can be a design element in a jewelry project, not just the base piece. Chain dangles add length to bead dangles and charms. Tassels are just several chain lengths on an eye pin. Try mixing different sizes, styles, and metal colors.

CHAIN NECKLACE

Approx. length: 34" excluding pendant

You'll need:

- large antique silver chain for necklace
- small black chain for bead dangles
- key pendant with attached charms and dangles
- assorted medium and large white and grey beads (we used 15)
- small, medium, and large antique silver jump rings
- antique silver head pins
- chain-nose pliers (2 pair), round-nose pliers, and wire cutters

Read Jewelry Making Basics, pages 4-13, before making your necklace.

To make the necklace:

1. Make 15 bead dangles ***(Figs. 1-3, pages 27-28)*** with the beads and head pins.
2. To make the chain dangles, cut 5 lengths of the small black chain, varying in length from 3/4" to 1 3/4". Make 5 long dangles by joining jump rings ***(Fig. 3, page 20)*** to the chains. Using the chain-nose pliers, join the bead dangles to the chains ***(Photo 1)***.

Photo 1

Continued on page 36.

CHAIN NECKLACE continued

3. Cut a 36" length and a 1" length of the large chain.
4. Use a large jump ring to connect both ends of the 36" chain. Attach the 1" chain length and the long dangles to the large jump ring ***(Photo 2)***.
5. Use a large jump ring to attach the pendant to the 1" chain length.
6. Use the medium jump rings to attach the remaining bead dangles to the necklace.

Photo 2

GLASS TEARDROP EARRINGS

You'll need:

- 2 large glass teardrop beads
- 2 large brown acrylic beads
- 4 small bronze crystal beads
- antique copper chain
- 2 antique copper ear wires
- 2 antique copper eye pins
- 2 large antique copper jump rings
- chain-nose pliers (2 pair), round-nose pliers, and wire cutters

Read Jewelry Making Basics, pages 4-13, before making your earrings.

For each earring:

1. Cut 3 chain lengths, each about $2^1/_4$," varying the lengths just a bit. Use a jump ring ***(Fig. 3, page 20)*** to attach the chain lengths to a teardrop bead.
2. To make the beaded connector, thread 2 crystal beads and an acrylic bead on an eye pin. Make a loop ***(Figs. 1-3, pages 31-32)*** at the wire end ***(Photo 1)***.

Photo 1

3. Use the chain nose pliers to attach the connector to the ear wire.
4. Use the jump ring to attach the tear drop bead to the connector.

ANGEL WING NECKLACE

Approx. length: 29", excluding pendant

You'll need:

- silver angel wing pendant with attached chain dangles
- pink circle medallion with center opening
- assorted medium pink, silver, and gold beads
- monogram interchangeable charm
- small silver chain
- 32" length of narrow pink ribbon
- silver head pins
- silver jump rings
- chain-nose pliers, round-nose pliers, and wire cutters

Read Jewelry Making Basics, pages 4-13, before making your necklace.

Continued on page 40.

To make the necklace:

1. Thread a 2" chain length through the circle medallion. Attach a jump ring ***(Fig. 3, page 20)*** to the chain ends.
2. Make 3 bead dangles ***(Figs. 1-3, pages 27-28)*** using the beads and eye pins. Attach chain lengths to the dangles as desired. Attach the chains to the medallion jump ring ***(Photo 1)***.
3. Use a jump ring to attach the medallion to the wing pendant. Attach a jump ring to the top of the pendant. Attach the monogram charm to the pendant.
4. Thread the ribbon through the pendant jump ring. Thread both ribbon ends through a few beads. Knot the ribbon ends together.

Photo 1

USING CONES

Multiple strands of beads threaded together through metal cones make for a lovely piece of jewelry. The cones hide the eye pin that holds the beaded strands together, giving the piece a polished look.

GLASS PENDANT NECKLACE

Approx. length: 32", excluding pendant

Read Jewelry Making Basics, pages 4-13, before making your necklace.

You'll need:

- glass pendant
- brown, amber, and yellow seed beads
- 56" length of sheer gold ribbon
- 2 bronze cones
- 2 bronze eye pins
- 3 bronze large oval jump rings
- bronze nylon-coated beading wire
- bronze crimp beads and crimp tool
- beading thread and beading needle
- jeweler's glue
- chain-nose pliers (2 pair), round-nose pliers, and wire cutters
- spring bead stop

To make the necklace:

1. Cut three 16" wire lengths. Use crimp beads ***(Figs. 1-3, page 24)*** to attach the wire lengths to the loop of an eye pin ***(Fig. 1)***. Thread the seed beads on the wires until the beaded sections are 12" long each, using the spring bead stop to temporarily secure the beads. Use a crimp bead to attach an eye pin to the loose wire ends.

Fig. 1

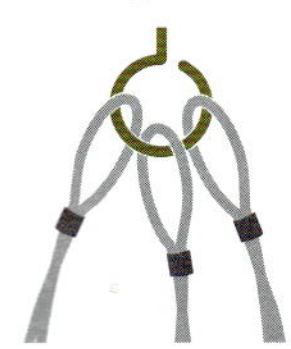

Continued on page 42.

GLASS PENDANT NECKLACE continued

2. Thread the eye pins through the wide end of the cones. Make a loop at each wire end ***(Figs. 1-3, pages 27-28)*** and attach a jump ring ***(Fig. 3, page 20)*** to each loop.
3. To make the beaded pendant bail, place a bead stop on a 16" length of beading thread ***(Fig. 2)***. Thread seed beads on the beading thread for 4". Remove the bead stop. Tie the thread with a surgeon's knot ***(Fig. 3)***, forming a ring. Apply a drop of glue to the knot. Once dry, trim the thread ends.
4. Double the beaded bail and attach to the pendant with a jump ring. Slide the pendant on the necklace.
5. Cut the ribbon in half. Fold and knot a ribbon length through each jump ring. Knot the ribbon ends together.

Fig. 2

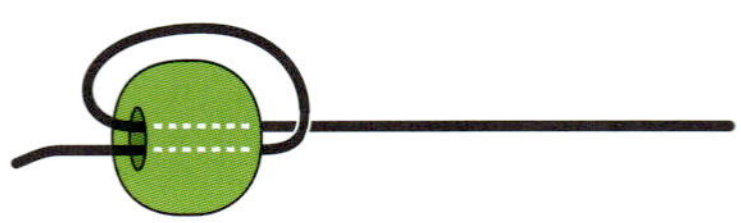

Fig. 3

BEADED BRACELET

You'll need:

- ◆ assorted medium beads (we used 33)
- ◆ thin cord or very narrow ribbon to coordinate with beads
- ◆ 2 silver cones
- ◆ silver toggle clasp
- ◆ 2 silver jump rings
- ◆ 2 silver eye pins
- ◆ chain-nose pliers, round-nose pliers, and wire cutters

Read Jewelry Making Basics, pages 4-13, before making your bracelets.

To make the bracelet:

1. Cut two 12" lengths of cord.
2. Tie one end of each cord to an eye pin. Thread the eye pin through a cone ***(Fig. 1)***. Make a loop ***(Figs. 1-3, pages 27-28)*** at the eye pin end. Attach one end of the clasp using a jump ring ***(Fig. 3, page 20)*** .

Fig. 1

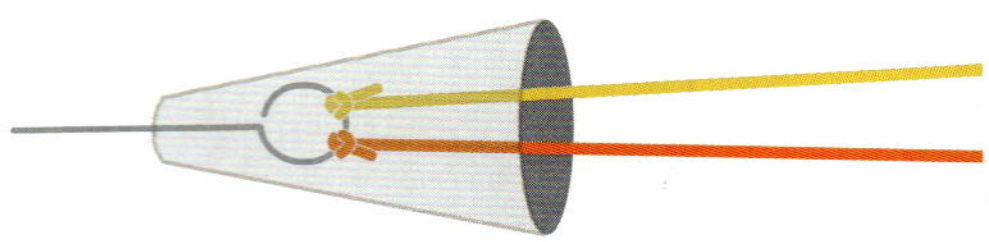

3. Thread the beads on the cords. Adjust the length as necessary by adding or removing beads.
4. Repeat Step 2 to attach the remaining clasp end.

MAKING PENDANTS

Many times you just can't find the right pendant for a necklace. The ready-made pendants are too small, not the right shape, or not quite the right color. Well, make your own by combining beads and other jewelry components!

AMBER PENDANT NECKLACE

You'll need:

- velvet cord 18" necklace
- large amber acrylic gemstone
- 6 white/brown metal-lined glass beads
- 4 amber jeweled spacer beads
- assorted small beads, metal spacers, and silver/rhinestone spacers for pendant
- silver bail
- silver nylon-coated beading wire
- silver crimp bead and crimp tool
- wire cutters

Read Jewelry Making Basics, pages 4-13, before making your necklace.

Continued on page 48.

AMBER PENDANT NECKLACE continued

To make the necklace:

1. For the pendant, thread a 12" wire length through a very small bead. With the bead centered on the wire, fold the wire in half and thread the small beads, spacers, and gemstone on the wire ***(Fig. 1)***. Use a crimp bead ***(Figs. 1-3, page 24)*** to attach the wire ends to the bail ***(Fig. 2)***.

Fig. 2

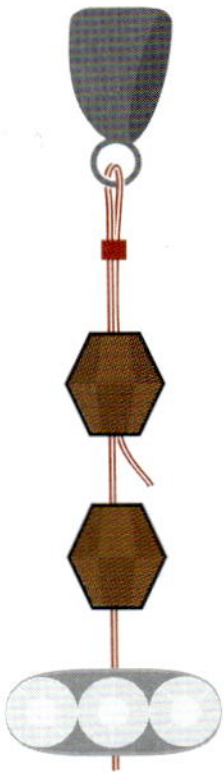

Fig. 1

2. String the remaining beads, spacers, and pendant on the necklace.